THE TRUTH IS

Desperate Times Calls for Desperate Faith

MARIE A. TURNER

authorHOUSE®

AuthorHouse™
1663 Liberty Drive
Bloomington, IN 47403
www.authorhouse.com
Phone: 1 (800) 839-8640

Published by AuthorHouse 06/10/2016

ISBN: 978-1-5246-1316-7 (sc)
ISBN: 978-1-5246-1315-0 (e)

Library of Congress Control Number: 2016909401

Print information available on the last page.

This book is printed on acid-free paper.

Table of Contents

Introduction

For as far back in my life that I can remember I have always tried to be independent. I was raised to work hard and achieve goals. I recall my parents as loving and patient as they are always instilling in us that "baby if you want it you have to work hard for it!" I have always had a desire to be a blessing to others. I certainly enjoy the feeling of seeing someone's spirits being lifted; that feeling alone changes the dynamics of your circumstance. I watched my parents give, down through the years, even when they did not have. They took people into our home and loved them in spite of our circumstances, or the individuals they trusted God to supply our needs. Often we say, "When I become an adult I will never do the things that my parents did," but whatever is in you will come out.

Whatever happens in life, don't block its flow; it's all essential to where we are going in our future. Remember the word of Jeremiah 29:11; "He knows the plans He has for us." We never want to find ourselves in a place of complacency when we think about how marvelous God has been to us. He's such a way maker! In our youth, enough was never enough. Our parents would say, "You always have your hand out for more!" Absolutely correct, we didn't value family in our youth but with the way that this world is set up, we should be honored to have values that last. Having warm meals, clothing, shelter, family dinners, family prayers, these values last! How do we get back to the basics, how do we get these values back into our homes, our schools, and our marriages?

In this book, *The Truth Is*, I want us all to evaluate our lives and our values, and determine what is more important. We are living in such perilous times, and people are dying every day. We hear of tragedies, and of loved ones that are perfectly healthy expiring without warning. Why do we have a problem with loving and forgiving? *The Truth Is*, love while you can, laugh all you can, cherish moments while you can, be sweet, be kind, and always ask the question: "What Would Jesus Do?" *The Truth Is,* He loves unconditionally!

Foreword

To my amazing mother, who has inspired many. I admire you and I love you because of the woman you are. Your wisdom, your bravery, your humble and calm spirit speaks volumes of your character. I have only watched you grow and push forward while remaining optimistic when everything didn't always look good. You have remained supportive to me and many others. You have always made time to be there when it counted most. I appreciate you so much for that. I have no clue what I'd do without you. All these years you have worked so hard and many have looked on the outside but don't truly know your story. FINALLY, you have the chance to share with the world your life story. This only part one to your series. So everyone stay tuned because Marie Turner is just beginning. I love you mommy, I am beyond grateful to have been birthed from a remarkable and astonishing woman as yourself. Keep pushing girlfriend!

—Love Booter

To my daughter Marie this has been an amazing journey we've shared together. Through many ups and downs the Lord has always been by your side. There were times when people said that you would never make it, but you held on to your dreams with your head up high. Yes, the road was rough, many doors were closed, but you kept your vision before you and God answered your prayers. I remember the many long hours you worked into the morning when you got your first small building, but those were great moments of fun, that made everyone feel like family. You didn't just enjoy doing hair, you were passionate about touching people's lives each time they sat in your chair. You always wanted your customers to be comfortable and you spared no expenses even if it was your rent money. There were times I would even say "Lord how are you going to fix this" and you would say, "The Lord will make a way!" Your salon became a healing station for those who were hurting and the Lord would give you words of encouragement, for each customer's situation.

The Lord does all things well and He knew there was greater inside you. Each client you served was your training ground for the ministry, God would later birth in you. To see you standing today as a business owner and Pastor is amazing. You've passed every test even when you could not see the light at the end of the tunnel. Although many of your dreams have been fulfilled, your journey is not over, it's just beginning! There are greater and more wonderful things that the Lord has in store for you. Stay the humble person you are and continue to let your good shine forth. I am looking forward to this new chapter in your life.

—Doris Fooks

Marie Turner's book The Truth Is, an encouraging book that teaches us that through all seasons of our lives we must always trust God. In this book Marie gives us life experiences that teach us how important it is to stay humble and to listen to God's still voice. She has captured the essence of love, heart ache, joy, disappointment, faith, trust, and peace. A must read, you will be inspired and know that all things are possible with God. The truth is you will have a deeper understanding that His plans for your life is better than any plan that you can imagine, regardless of your circumstances. Thank you for being transparent and allowing God to use your life as an open book to be a blessing to others.

—Kaveen Coulbourne

Marie A. Turner is woman of integrity, authenticity and great wisdom. Gifted and anointed, funny and charismatic, classy and down-to-earth, Marie has a heart of compassion and a desire to see the kingdom of God manifested in the earth and in the lives of God's people. She is sold out to God, refuses to compromise His word, and stands firm in her faith. Her life is a living testimony of the manifested promises of God, the courage it takes to not only follow Him but to stand flatfooted, unwavering and unmoved on His word. This book is God-inspired, and I am convinced that as you read it, ingest it and allow it to take root and grow, the words will transform your life, change your thinking and dramatically alter how you see yourself. She will help you understand that your life has meaning, purpose and that God has a set time for the plans He has for your life. As you read each chapter, you will laugh, you will cry, but ultimately it will confirm that God is not slack concerning His promises towards you. Despite the obstacles, setbacks, and disappointments, Marie A. Turner stayed the course, didn't give up and held tight to the promises of God.

She is walking into her destiny and this book is proof that God has a plan, purpose and mission for your life as well that only you can fulfill.

—Dr. Nina Lyon Bennett
New Beginning Covenant Ministries
Salisbury, MD

Special Thanks

First, I need to thank my Lord and Savior for all He has ever done for me, without him, I could do nothing! I want to thank God for my parents, Bishop Robert Fooks Sr. and Lady Doris Fooks; they have been my motivation and my biggest cheerleaders. My wonderful husband of 23 years, Kaile. He is my best friend, my lover, my prayer partner, my soulmate, my covering, the father of our four awesome children, a Pop Pop, a Godfather, a mentor, and friend to so many. I salute you, baby! Staci has been a jewel of a daughter. She has been my motivation to finish this book. Kaile, my handsome young man, is growing so strong and independent. Kasie, my sweet young lady and is Mommy's personal prophetess. Tyson, my handsome son, who came in on the latter end and is making his mark in our family, and Taylor, the sweetest little princess you would ever want to know. Keniyah, the little lady the Lord sent into my life. Godchildren, Cameron and Jourdyn, I love you. To my siblings, Robert, Tracey and Corethea, thank you for always believing in my dream; and to my New and Living Way (NALW) church family, Mr. and Mrs. Hearn, aunts, uncles and other family and friends. To God be the glory for the things He has done!

A special "thank you" to my editor, Carolyn Friend; and my book coach, Teresha Sutton.

Special Thanks

[illegible] Lord and Savior for all He has [illegible] done for me [illegible] [illegible] thankful [illegible] I want to [illegible]

[illegible]

[illegible] the things He has done [illegible]

[illegible] special thanks [illegible] my book cover, Teresa Sutton.

Chapter 1

The Cover Up

"When you take time with God and listen to his voice, he renews your strength and enables you to handle life" (author unknown).

There are deep secrets in all of us that we do not desire for anyone to know. We spend a portion of each day covering up the flaws in our lives. Therefore, to others, it appears that we have it all together. All along, we are hiding, masking, and making it look good on the outside. While on the inside, there is misery, pain, and disappointment. Then there is another side to it all. Some people put you in a position where they see your outer, but have no idea what it takes even for you to smile, get dressed and put on your best. We live in a world where people place you by the things you obtain in life without ever really knowing who you are. When we were children, my parents owned their own business. My Dad did so well that I never knew about any type of struggle. Back then, parents kept things from their children. It is important that we become transparent and that our children know that life happens.

My teachers and friends perceived in their minds that the Fooks children were wealthy. To realize that we are all the Kings Kids is to know automatically we are wealthy. Nevertheless, the catch to it all is as Paul says to the Corinthian church, "I know how to abase and abound," meaning I know what it's like to have lots and to have little. We all have valley experiences. It is not the valley that is bad, but it's how you go through the valley that determines your level of victory. We are pleased when things are smooth with no bumps in the road and our homes, and our jobs are great. We are in a place where our children are obedient, and we are living behind the white picket fence; that all sounds well and dandy.

However, there comes a time where our faith is tried and we become weak along the way. We must look to Jesus, who is the author and finisher of our faith. God strategically places us in experiences so His glory can be revealed. Look at Job, the test of all tests came his way. Imagine losing everything, but still having faith to know that no matter what my God cannot fail! That's enough to make you run laps around the house, come back, sip some water and watch God fight your battle, even in the face of your enemy.

So many times in my walk I have wanted to cover my face and say "what's the use," but there's a level of fight inside of each of us, even when you want to give up you have to trust the process. I am so glad God can trust me with the trial even when it hurts. I wanted to run and hide so many times, but God gave me a warriors praise that made me see every crooked place straight. I have seen the Lords ability do the abundant in my life, even when things seemed impossible. I have recognized my own personal worth, it's not always easy to smile and give to others, the same ones you sacrifice for, those that have spoken negatively of you, all the while leaving you for dead, and you have given them your last. However, the word says, "I have never seen the righteous forsaken nor his seed begging bread." It is always good to be true to yourself so you can really be true to others.

Listen my friend; it is never good to cover up how you feel to appease someone else's feelings. Some days you need personal time and some days you need someone to encourage you. Not every day is not going to be a mountain top experience. There would be days I would have to push myself, remember who I am and who I belong to. If He could carry my mess all the way to the cross so I could live, the least I could do is keep up the good fight of faith. My Savior is a deliverer. I am living proof of that. It is so much easier to be yourself than to be someone that God never intended you to be. Happiness is a choice, not a mandate, but with happiness comes peace and with peace comes joy. Life does come with failures so don't try to get away from them. Use them to grow and don't be disheartened. Use trials to help someone else avoid the same disappointments. We can't save folk from everything, but we can sure share. It's what we do with our failures that help us recognize our worth. Shake yourself, speak to yourself, learn from it, move forward and breathe new life. Don't ever cover up who you are, expose yourself to the truth; there is more gratitude with having a positive attitude.

Your Thoughts

Chapter 2

The Spirit of Intimidation

"Knowing yourself is the beginning of all wisdom" (author unknown).

The Cambridge dictionary's definition of "intimidation" is to frighten or threaten someone usually in order to persuade him or her to do what he or she does not desire. Intimidation is also called a spirit because truly that's what it is when someone or something tries to control us. Oftentimes people, places, and things can intimidate us and move us directly outside of our comfortable, normal behavior and that's terrible! No one wants to be around anyone or anything that makes us feel uncomfortable! When you walk into a room or meet someone for the first time, and you feel, I can't be me, or if you have to pretend to be something you are not, it's absolutely not the environment for you! Run and take cover. We only want to surround ourselves with people that are going to make us better and bring out the best in us. Know your self-worth. Let's not ever put on a façade or a mask. It is so hard to be a counterfeit, but it's a pleasure to be original. We say this at our church all the time when people say they are so unhappy, or they feel like they don't fit in. Really? Or I'm going to leave. Really? Remember, you carry yourself wherever you go, so running is not the answer. They have the same issues in South Africa that we have here in Salisbury, so you have to know your worth. Never let anyone or anything run you away from your blessings. That same spirit will be there if you are not secure in you! God is so awesome He always tells us we are fearfully and wonderfully made. Psalms 139:14. So listen, your environment does not change you or define you! You change and define your surroundings by your presence, and you become the difference you want to see. That's why the Lord commands us to love as He first loved us, John 3:16. He loved us so much He gave us love to give love, to shift the atmosphere to be one of love. So the game does not change us, we change the game. That is why we are still here and did not die from it but thrived through it. You earned this place; you suffered for this, so why allow your surroundings to dictate to you.

I have been in some major circumstances. I almost allowed my own insecurities to talk me out of my rewards and my blessings. People sure can make you feel bad when God does something great for you. On the other hand, sometimes it is the moment you get to know you, the moment you defeat the odds, the day you smile instead of cracking, that moment that you get that "aha" and gain new strength. That is the moment you realized you have fought for this smile; you have fought for this praise; don't you dare stare me down and try to rob me of this victory. I am shouting, to God be the glory! Lord, you rock!

As I am writing I began to think of how things are developed in our youth; train up a child in the way they should go and when they get older they will not depart. Proverbs 22:6. We should think about the ones that look up to us and admire us. When I was a young girl, I had mentors, those I admired, and my parents who were the best example that a girl could ever ask for. As I was growing and developing, they allowed me to grow into my own identity. I started learning so much about myself. It's a great thing for a parent to allow their child to grow. What's bad is that sometimes we have made bad choices in our youth, but what is put in, will come out. Now I am an adult with my own babies, and I am still learning every day who I am. It is a process. I dislike it when folk act as if they have arrived because we are always learning. Everyday it is something new, even with my hubby. It's been nearly 30 years, and we are still learning each other, discovering and growing together.

A hilarious memory was when I was in high school:

> *I was skinny, no boobs, flat tummy, thick black uncontrollable hair, and extremely hairy legs. My teammates would make fun of me, "Marie your legs are gross." I loved sports, so to fit in and not be talked about, I had to make some moves. My arms were hairy; I wore a monkey look for a couple of years until 11th grade. (Thanks, Daddy! That came from you, laughs).*

Can you imagine me being bold and carefree? Remember that the intimidation spirit can make you do what you don't want to now and then. When I became a young bride, my hubby loved my hairy legs, yet there are some that still look at me as if I have a disease. Even going to buy shoes was a task when the salesperson would look at my legs, I would say to myself, here we go again. After years of folk looking at me funny, I was forced to shave, and ladies it's such a chore; something else for me to add to my daily regimen. Now, I do love the look but let's say; now I do it for me. So, I say to my hairy sisters if you like it own it. Have your own mind. It is ok to feel inspired but keep your inspiration real. Being intimidated is a terrible feeling. Be true to yourself and you can be true to others. Even in our spiritual commitment as leaders, there are times when we are pushed or groomed to follow someone else's footsteps, which is all well and good. But remember to stay true to the call God gave you. We are all different, and we articulate differently. Respect yourself and you will know how to respect others. Remember this; always treat someone the way you desire to be treated. Let's defeat the enemy of intimidation.

Your Thoughts

Chapter 3

Fear of Failure

"God will never leave you empty. He will replace everything you lost. If he asks you to put something down, it's because he wants you to pick up something greater" (unknown).

Failure: lack of success! Nobody in this world wants to feel like they are useless. We were all born for a purpose, and it's up to us to reach deep and cultivate the gifts that God has given us.

II Timothy 1:6 admonishes us to stir up the gifts. What is in you? What have you not done due to the spirit of fear? Think about it every great person has been given the chance to either excel or give up. Life is about choice. God has not given us the spirit of fear, but power, love, and a sound mind. II Timothy 1:7. Wow! How amazing! We have all been given a measure of faith. Activate it and work what you have until you get what you want! Have you ever heard the phrase failure is not an option? Well, that is true and false. Again, we have the power of choice, and God has given that to us' He doesn't force us. We have to be willing. Can you imagine being in a relationship that you are forced to love someone? Not me!

There's another phrase that I have heard; life is like a rollercoaster sometimes it is up, down, happy times, and sad times. Seasons come and go, some are good, and some we never desire to revisit. Overall, it's what you make of it. Be strong and be very vigilant! The dreams that we are given are sometimes stronger than our desires.

I believe that God reveals many things to us through our dreams. Have you ever had a dream that felt so real like you were actually living in that moment? That dream felt so real; you did not want to wake up! So let's compare the two. I actually asked a few of my sisters which one outweighed the other, so let's see what the dictionary says about dreams. Dreams are a series of thoughts, images, and sensations occurring in a person's mind during sleep. Our desires are strong feelings of wanting to have something or wishing for something to happen! Let's look at it this way, because honestly it's a matter of opinion. I have always dreamed of having a facility that can house families in crisis. When we go through life's struggles, sometimes we are frowned upon as if we did something wrong but understand, life happens. Often things are out of our control. Can you imagine going through a storm and being treated unfairly? Well, unfortunately, that's how cruel society can be. We are blessed to be a blessing!

Dreams can be captivating. I can imagine myself helping ladies and gents with hair loss. I dream of being able to service them even when they do not have the resources. Now I look at this not only to be helpful, but I desire not to go into debt doing so! The reality of it is you have to have the finances to get things done. Sometimes we are restricted by reality, but who can stop a girl from dreaming? I don't dream of a bigger home or cars. We have a roof over our head and decent vehicles to drive, but there is always that but. Let's find joy and excitement in dreaming. Don't take me from it, let me live in the moment until it's no longer a dream but a reality. "Whew" I feel this thing as I am typing! Now, we cannot always share our dreams (Joseph) because there are dream killers and dream snatchers who will slap you right out of a great moment with their "what ifs."

There have been times in my life that I have allowed the distractions of the enemy to deposit thoughts of failure in me. I am absolutely saved, yes, I am, do I love Jesus, yes, I do. But I am human, so I have allowed my own personal "what ifs" to block my flow, have you? Are you afraid; are you uncertain how things will pan out for you? Are you wondering where the resources are coming from to finish what you have started! How about this, just get started. Just get up and get to moving. Let's go deeper! When God sees us doing our part He knows we are serious. Let me say this to encourage you; do it the way God wants you to. Let's not compare ourselves; that's a set up for failure! Let me give you a quote from Napoleon Hill "he who fears being conquered is sure of defeat." So on the flip side of things; the Bible says in Romans 8:3-39 we are more than conquers. Therefore, everything I need, God has already done! Yes Lord, yes I get it now! If I am on the mountain, you are there, in the valley, you are there also. You are my friend. Thanks, Lord you have me. In other words, when I do not even have myself you have me covered. When my enemies come in like a flood, you are there. Yes God! Are you getting this as I am right now? That's a good place to put a praise! Napoleon says it like this: "to do all that one is able to, is to be man; to do all that one would like to do is to be God." So champions, we cannot fail we are children of the King!

Your Thoughts

Chapter 4

The Family

"When you feel a peaceful joy that's when you are near truth" (Rumi).

I am certainly a country girl. I grew up in the city of Mardela Springs (ha-ha). My parents are well loved by many. I have three siblings, and we were raised to love God with our whole heart! My parents took precious time teaching us in our youth how to pray and recite Bible verses. My Dad never sent us out of the house without early morning prayer. It is so essential to a healthy life! Our home was always filled with love, good food, discipline, and lots of laughter. My Mom was so cool, and still is; we are teaching her in her senior years to be hip.

So, why do you think things are so different now with families? Why is there so much division in families? Why do people keep secrets that can be harmful to their future? Well to be truthful, it started with our society. When we were coming up, if you showed your tail it was dealt with right then. Now parents are afraid to give their children a good old fashion spanking because the moment you do, it can be your fate. You mean to tell me that our children can now run our homes; the home you have worked hard for, denied yourself for, just to make sure they have food, clothing, shelter, money for school, clothes, and field trips, and you can't even get a thank you. Oh no saints. Joshua 8:31 says "as for me and my house we are going to serve the Lord." Yep, that's a fact! I am so blessed to be able to have such an awesome legacy that can be passed down to my babies.

I remember growing up and not appreciating what I had in my parents. I thought they were strict. Child, don't let us girls even think about bringing home a young man that wasn't saved, you could forget that. When I turned fifteen, love came. Now I had boyfriends before but none like this love. Y'all know exactly what young love was like. You would do anything to be with each other. Well look, this nice looking guy with pretty brown eyes looked at me, and I looked at him and said: "well this is it!" Oh yeah, I failed to mention my Mom hooked us up. Back in our day, Skateland was the spot. Raised in a holiness church, going to Skateland was like going to the club to the Saints but not for my Momma. She took us and hung out with us. She played hopscotch and double dutch. That is why everyone loved our home. It was the spot for all the cousins, and we were bad! Yes, I said it terrible! Who plays hide and go get it with their cousins, or kiss tag. Well, we did. We traveled with my parents on summer vacations; that was normal for us. Our family was our world, and being with family creates lasting values and memories.

My brother and I were inseparable. Oh, how I love him. He would protect me and take care of his little sisters. Being the only boy, he had it hard. He didn't want us to get beatings so he would cover for us until our parents got hip to the game. We take these things lightly, but when is the last time you told your family you loved them? When was the last time you hugged them? When is the last time you spent valuable time together? Are you holding grudges and unforgiveness in your heart? If so, do you know that every day you do not forgive is one last day you have to live? It's like a plague eating at your soul. If you do not forgive your brothers and sisters, how do you expect your heavenly Father to forgive you? That's the Word, Matthew 6:15. We should ask God to forgive us today for not forgiving. Oh, how I honestly adore God. He is certainly our bridge; He's our mediator. Let him bridge every gap, break every curse, bind the hand of the enemy; makes him look crazy not you.

I ask God to keep our family bond all the time. I told my son; "I said we are not perfect, far from it, but we have love." My husband has been such an excellent example of love to me. When the king of your castle roars, he combats the enemy like a lion. It's been almost 30 years for us. As I said earlier, I fell in love at fifteen. Well honey listen, it turns out it wasn't puppy love but that good love. Hey! Bring your minds in! It's the love that only God ordained for husbands and wives. Today rebuke the adversary and evict him from your family, your marriage, your finances, and serve him notice that he cannot abide there anymore. Every family has issues. Every young girl dreams of having a home, children, a handsome husband, good paying job, money in the bank, and elaborate trips, but that is not reality.

Life is family. Imperfect but perfect. Why did I say that? Well, Little House on the Prairie was one of my favorite shows growing up. Let me tell you when I became a woman with a hubby and children; I was trying to figure out how to balance it all. That's why earlier I said I thank God for my husband. He is the glue that holds us together. He spoils this old girl. I was a workhorse, very focused on what I thought was important, all the while missing out on so much. It took me many years to see clearly. Don't miss it friend, do all you can. Build family values and create memories that last. When I just take a minute to reflect, I just want to tell God thank you for not cutting me off for my shortcoming. It is not always worldly things; it's those little things we don't even recognize. Don't count me out Lord. Growing up we used to sing: "Lord don't let me fail, I want to be your bride."

My Godmother said something very profound to me about family, dreams, goals, and the things we desire for our family. Some things seem so unobtainable, but by faith, they are obtained. I have always desired for my children to be greater than us and I'm quite sure my parents wanted the same for thing for us. That's why they worked hard. Society makes it so that we have to work extra hard to keep what we have, and in the meantime, we are missing out. Less is best, but that comes with time and wisdom.

The more you obtain the harder you have to work to maintain. My Daddy owned Fooks Hauling when I was growing up. Lord knows, folk thought we were rich. Hun listens, he would say when we missed the bus, "I will take you to school." Well listen, some days I wanted to walk. We looked like Sanford and Son. Daddy would have cars on the back of his truck and scrap metal, and we would get greasy getting out of there. Did I mention people could hear us before they could see us? How about this: we would get up early Saturday mornings because Dad was a military man. He would holler up the stairs "Reveille, Reveille (military term), all hands up. Feet hit the deck! I'm going take you guys shopping." Don't ever tell a girl she's going shopping; she gets ready in a flash. However, not before our rooms were spotless and the kitchen and the yard were clean. There were no dust balls allowed in the Fooks camp! You mention shopping, and you get all of our attention. With excitement and zeal, we would load up in our family Ford station wagon to go downtown to the Bargain Box. Daddy would say "you all can get whatever you like." Ba-ha-ha-ha that was funny to me. Folk assumed we were rich, but we were balling on a budget hard in the 80s'. We would come back home to the smell of Mom's fried chicken throughout the house. To top it all off, we would have friends over, and Mom never said a word. Nevertheless, that chick was like Jesus; she would take a little and feed a multitude. Aaah family! Do you have memories? That's good stuff right there!

Your Thoughts

Chapter 5

The Church

"God has placed you where you're at in this very moment for a reason. Remember that and trust he is working everything out" (unknown).

I want to start with who are we, and what have we become. I get very emotional when I think of how far the church has strayed away from the foundation and the values that have been imputed to us down through the years. We are called to serve not to be served. Matthew 20:28 says it best, "For even the Son of man came not to be served but to serve others, and to give his life as a ransom for many." What are we doing? Are we servants? I am so appalled at the fact that everybody wants a title, but no one wants to show love and kindness. I want to love; I want to see people free of bondage and chains. Why walk around bound when you can be free? He has paid the price for our redemption. I don't want to preach, but I want to live a life that preaches a sermon that will cause freedom. I grew up in church, it's in my DNA, and God knows I am grateful for my foundation! Nevertheless, I need to be transparent with you all. Folk do not want church, nor do they want a program. They want an encounter that will change the very dynamics of their lives. I want realness, not a fancy car or gator shoes.

Man listen, I will never ever forget how bad I was hurt in church. I was talked about and laughed at. Some said it didn't take all that, sit her down. Whew, that is why I am so blessed to have parents that put some good stuff in me! "Keep your head up; we are going to make it." These are the words that my Dad said to me when I found out I was pregnant at the age of nineteen. Oh yeah, I was saved and sneaking and creeping but child listen, your sins will expose you! I certainly was not married; I was Holy Ghost filled and fire baptized, but I was doing my thing! I must say that sometimes the older saints forget where they have come from, or where they are hiding from and not being truthful about their shortcomings. He is such a forgiving and strong God.

Let me tell you why I decided to hang in there: giving in was not an option. If I didn't know anything else, I knew that He loved me with my flaws. My brokenness became my wholeness. If you surrender your weaknesses, the Potter wants to put us back together again, yes He does. This is so why we can't do church, but we have to do deliverance. We have to empower, which is why we have to speak life, when it looks dim, dark, and done. Why in the world do you think the scripture says "lift up your head oh ye gates and be lifted up ye everlasting doors and the King will come in" Psalms 24:9. Hallelujah to the King! Thanks for loving me when I was counted out. Try relationship, try fellowship and see if you don't get peace. That joy will come. When you change your perspective, your outcome changes. I am here. I survived. Don't cry. Don't die. Live! We all make mistakes. Pick yourself up. Speak to yourself and say self, let's go.

Let's try this again. If He redeemed me, I am free! Let me say this; I think that God sits back and says, "What are my children doing?" If I can love the unlovable, I need them to duplicate my actions. My Dad was the youth minister at our family church in Mardela. He was such a fireball and all the youth loved him! Dad never judged, he loved, inspired, and motivated us to greatness. I really feel we need to get back to the basics of what matters most.

I know someone will say there has to be a standard, and baby, there are standards. Not just man made rules. How about just having order? We are living in a time that this generation needs to see it in the Word. Do you remember when we were young? We were not allowed to go to the movies, wear nail polish, or play basketball. The saints of old would say that's worldly. I will never forget my Mom took us out of pants because our pastor at the time said we should not wear anything pertaining to a man. It's cold outside Ma. Ok, we will get you girls some leg warmers. Honey, you and I both know it was frigid outside so, what did we do? Became sneaky! I recall waiting until Mommy would go to work and we would go behind the house while waiting on the bus and put on our pants. The neighbors, who happened to be our grandparents, would tell on us every time. I am so glad that season passed, and Mom came to herself. My Mother was from Southeast D.C. She didn't normally let the Saints bully her, but she said my girls are not going to hell over pants. Thanks Mom! Thanks!

Some of this stuff is foolishness y'all. If the Lord were so concerned about our outward appearance, some of us would not make it for just being ugly. Ba-ha-ha-ha not literally, but your actions alone make you ugly. For all you deep folk we're talking figuratively and not literally.

Now with that being said, ya'll stop judging folks and start loving them. What would Jesus do?

Let's not be so busy being busy that we miss God. He's about to transition your life to greatness. He's about to turn your mourning into dancing. Somebody really should praise God for where you are going, and thank God for where you have been. It's my past that makes me embrace my future. It makes me rejoice that He brought me out, and He kept me. I am not crazy; I am a conquer! Hello, you are too! The Bible says "we are more than." "Listen Linda listen, the people of God are moving forward.

The real people of God are shifting and pushing past our stuff and reaching for him. Can the real people of God please stand up? There's a clarion call going out to the body of Christ. God wants to see His warriors; He needs you. Yes, you, no one can do what you have been called to do, so stop trying to hand off your assignment. What in the world are you waiting on?

Get up, get motivated, and get dedicated. Hey, do you hear God calling you? Samuel, it's not Eli calling your name it is Jesus. He has work for you and a calling on your life.

If you would have told me 20 years ago that God was calling me to be a pastor, I would have laughed at you. If you had told my husband when he was in the world hanging with his boys, he would have said the same. But check this out; he peaked into our future Jeremiah 29:11. Whew! God has a plan with your name on it! To the flawed and the broken, Rise. To the drug dealer, Rise. To the girl sleeping with someone else's man, Rise. To the homeless, Rise. There shall be glory after this! The world needs you, the body of Christ needs you, and I need you. We need what you are working with. Have you ever wondered why, when you were in your mess, and you should have been cut off, dead, handicapped, or crazy, and that you have been kept? He is a keeper; He is a mind regulator. He is God and God alone. Brother and sister live.

Your Thoughts

Chapter 6

The Bondage

"God's plans will always be greater and more beautiful than all your disappointments" (unknown).

This is the hardest part of my story. This is where it all began for me, my God! The truth hurts, but being transparent makes us free. So, let me begin this chapter by saying this: we began to deal with dreams earlier, and sometimes when our potential is recognized, we tend to become vulnerable. With great excitement, I had a dream. I began to envision myself in my own salon after renting for so long, with so many obstacles and many battles to fight. We had a good team that really had our best interest at heart. We were pulled upon day and night. So many times, we see the outcome, but we clearly do not understand all that has to be put into the vision. I believe that is why Paul admonishes us not to grow weary in our well doing. Galatians 6:9. There is a season of reaping if we just hold on.

Many days I became overwhelmed, and there were days I wanted to say, that's all right. I wanted to change my mind because it was too much work, but I had to push. I had to fight. Please hold on to your seat, because what I am about to share with you is going to make you scream. I want you to know that nothing happens overnight. There are many disappointments, many tears shed, and many sleepless nights. With the help of God, I had to start my journey. Oprah Winfrey said it best "if you can't handle being talked about then you are not ready for success!" This is true. When I was in high school, I always dreamed of being a nurse. I loved helping people. I always wanted people to know that someone does care. We know that God sometimes has other plans.

I started off working in other salons. Then one day, after having my daughter Staci, I decided to go and work in my aunt's salon. Aunt Fannie opened her home and her wisdom to me, but I was young and dumb. Wise council is good if you take heed, but I wanted to do me, so I had to learn some things the hard way. I didn't have a manual or guide. I just had talent and faith.

I recall one day getting off work, and my auntie leads me into her kitchen to talk. "Rie Rie" (as my family and friends often call me) she said, you need your own. I'm taking your money, and this is your last week working with Aunt Fannie. I was perplexed. I had no business skill and no business degree, just talent and faith. Can you imagine how hurt I was? That day changed my life and would now lead me on a path to being a young black woman, with no working capital, trying to run my first salon! Ok, so where am I going to go, Lord? The way was already made. My parents were like Joshua and Caleb; they had already scouted out the land on Old Ocean City Road in Salisbury, a nice little spot in the middle of nowhere. This is the place where women would travel far and near just to receive service. Oh, did God meet us there? He will make a way in the wilderness. My clients loved me, and I loved them. We all became a big family and did I mention that everything I needed, God provided. From shampoo bowls to dryers, to products and towels.

Now the challenge would come, state board allowed me to go in but gave me a time to come up with a name. They allotted me time for inspection. Who does that except God? (Please no one try that now, times certainly have changed). My clients and I came up with a name "Extremities by Marie!" Wow and wow! So the conversation went a little like this. One of my customers at the time said, "Marie, you don't do anything regular but extreme." Shortly after, my Dad gave me a scripture that would remind me of where my help and guidance would come from when I grew weary. Can somebody say favor! The struggle Lord, the struggle. I worked long hours but for some reason, my clients stayed. We laughed, we cried, and we had church. Mom would watch their children, feed us, and give us wisdom on marriage and relationships. Mom was very involved in the business operation. She kept the money and would go after the clients that would try to sneak out and not pay. She ran errands and kept up with the finances.

Everything we needed, God provided. Somebody should help me dance! Let me say this: sometimes we would have no heat, we would be snowed in, but no one, and I mean nobody complained or left. Some days we were so crowded we didn't have room for parking or anything else. We had a small staff and a pleasant atmosphere, but we were busting out at the seams! It was time for a shift, and this would be one of many!

The God of all grace and wisdom gave us favor everywhere we would place our feet upon. Our staff was on board, as we proceeded forward. Route 50 West here we come! I'm trying to tell you we took over every territory. Folk was envious of us, but please tell somebody that may not know this, "if God is for you who can be against us!" This is another good place to praise! Listen, my friend, I didn't have a fat bank account, I didn't have anyone giving me big bucks, but God provided all my needs. All I had to do was speak it in faith, and God would cause it to manifest.

This is a sidebar, have you been waiting for something to happen? Then I hate to tell you this, as long as you are waiting and not moving, nothing will ever happen for you! James 2:20 tells us that faith without works is dead. Waiting is awesome, but if you waited for something to happen, chances are, it would not. Every farmer has to till the ground with the anticipation of a harvest. I love God because He first loved me, John 3:16 proves that. Remember when I said that I did not obtain a degree I mean this thing has been trial and error, ups and downs, failures and victories. Quote by Ritu Ghatourey says, "Every successful person has a painful story, and every painful story has a successful ending!" I am so blessed by the struggle, and I am glad that I tried. One could never know what they are truly capable of unless they try.

When we moved to a larger location, it was for more space, but don't you know the higher you go, the more trials come, more bills and more ridicule. I'm being polite. In our terms, the haters come; folk don't be praying they just talk. Thank you, Lord, for the haters, they have made me greater. He never promised me the way would be easy, but He promised me He would never leave me! My expenses gave me a fit by now. I found myself working extra just to keep the operation running.

I still had a great team at the time. God knows He kept us; water bills, electric, rent high as the sky, telephone, products, payroll, and the list go on. Did I mention that back then we were making $50 for a relaxer? Lord, somehow we made it!

Well, I signed a three-year lease, and I knew nothing about legal documents, I was just young and ambitious. To my surprise, each month the rent was growing. Ask me how? Well, I signed for $900 a month in rent but in the fine print, it stated that the occupant had to cover common area maintenance. Some months I was paying $1,800. Listen, Linda; that was extreme for us back then. Remember the average hairstyle was $25 but again, God did it! Well, I really wanted to be evicted, so I stopped paying and just put the money away. My Mom made sure of that! The property owner decided to take me to court. So I put on my professional attire so I would not be stereotyped. The judge was very nice, but he looked at me and said, "Ma'am you are liable, you signed the document; you have to pay." With tears in my eyes, shame and disappointment, we paid it and stayed the course. God knows I don't know how folks do shady stuff and get away with it or so it seems. God sustained us for the duration of time there and then it was time for round three.

Y'all moving again? Yes, we are. This time, we were beside the City Park, and I was so happy. Finally, relief, now we went about making it look like home. Tammy and I did it. She was such a trooper. My poor hubby helped by cleaning and doing towels while simultaneously working the night shift and being Mr. Mom. Remember, I was so inundated with the business, I missed valuable time with my children. Friend listen, the family is more important than a dollar bill! Lord knows I am a witness, but you live, you learn, and you grow. All seemed to be well; it seemed we were well liked, but all the while the people were scheming to get us out. Why? Because Extremities had too many clients. What in the world? Why this again, Lord? We go in and do what we are supposed to do. Now we are being persecuted for being busy! Oh, now we are being accused of taking up all the parking spaces, and the gossip court is saying our husbands are making passes at other women. Lord help us!

Now, six months into the lease, the property owner had someone walk in, hand me a paper, and walk out. To my surprise, it said, "You have 30 days to vacate the property." I'm thinking, "We pay on time, we are clean." Lord now where do we go in 30 days? Listen, I'm in full-blown tears, and I am not a crybaby! Please, somebody, say it's working for my good. They gave us a refund and our deposit back. I was about to be in another transition.

My client, Ms. Jesse Smiley, my English teacher in high school whom I love dearly, was livid by the accusations made. She was a strong advocate for the NAACP, and we were on our way to the media. I'm young, I'm black, I'm a woman, I'm blessed and the devil didn't like me. Ms. Smiley said, "Rie Rie you have rights, use them." Here I am mad to the bone. I was angry, and I wanted to tell the world how we were being treated. They did not even have the grounds to do what they did. The nerve of people always bullying us around! Then, I hear the Lord speaking, "stand still, and let me fight your battle!"

We win again! Another victory! No sooner than we got out of that building, it was on the news that the city of Salisbury was going to condemn it. Listen, God will protect his people. He covers us from dangers seen and unseen! You meant it for evil, but God meant it for good! It is time. Move Number Four.

Mrs. Jolley was a very warm and open person; the only problem was the Salon was over top of where she stored her hearses. Lord, thanks for providing. The clients didn't seem to care as long as we were all together and their hair was pretty and healthy. Certainly, God is faithful.

We laughed, we cried, we ran from the mice and the heat. I would be at work sometimes wanting to work in my birthday suit. This is too much! We would send codes when a man would come upstairs. Rie Rie was working in her brazier. It was hot; I can recall my client's hair sweating as fast as I was curling it. These moments were real. However, the moments, the trials, the good times, and the bad times made us. It didn't kill us! I remember one day it was 100 degrees outside and 110 inside, too funny, right? Lady Dickerson and Davina went marching their hips over to Mrs. J, and she said, "baby, I have some fans to help you girls out!" Are you ready for this? They came marching across the field with church fans. Ba-ha-ha. I love that little lady so. All jokes aside, with boldness, she said to me, "you need your own salon." Does that sound familiar? Aunt Fannie said those same words but this time Mrs. J. was speaking of me buying property. She set a fire down on the inside of me, and the truth is; I didn't want to hear those words of wisdom, but now I was forced to.

What if someone sees something in you before you see it or before you want to believe it? How about when you do not have the resources, and you felt you do not have enough collateral? Just let me say this, believe and have faith, it will come. You just move forward and watch God! It's about that time again, Move Number Five.

Mrs. J. provoked me to spy out the land and prepare to move. We had outgrown our space once again, and we really did need to move. God will make you uncomfortable in a place of comfort when it's time to move. Some of my customers were having trouble climbing the stairs, some even falling down the stairs. These are the same seniors that had been supporting us all these years so I had to make some accommodations. May I also add that all of a sudden, the same water that we had been using was now rusty. When the Lord gets ready, you have to move! I thought it would be best that while in the process of purchasing, I would merge our staff in with another salon. I really felt like we are doing well while going through the process of our purchase. Every time God is up to something big, the trial grows bigger. Let me just say this, my friend that we merged with got cold feet. Here today, and gone tomorrow. When I went into the salon, she had cleaned her station and was gone with the wind! At this point, I am nervous, God what do I do? Are the owners going to put us out? My name is not on the lease; I have no rights to this place! I decided I would just keep up the bills, even better, so no one would know but us. Remember, we are still in the process of buying. Lord, please grant us your favor. Please! He's so gracious, just let your request be known. What a marvelous God we serve.

The owner happened to be a very nice Doctor, certainly my God answers prayers. He allowed us to stay even with knowing we were in the process of purchasing our own. At the time, Dr. Carter and I worked together day and night as I stated earlier. She didn't let me give up, and she reminded me about Galatians 6:9, so I pushed. Let's have another transparent moment together. I had gotten so discouraged. Every dart that could come did come, and with a vengeance! Late one evening after Bible study, I decided to go to the Donut Connection (one of my stops almost every day), to get some crushed ice that I enjoyed. The Connection was down the street from our church, so it was a must! To my surprise, as I drove up to the window to get my ice and donuts for my babies, the little lady at the window was having a bad day. She decided to make me aware of it by throwing my money at me inside of my car! Whew, somebody say thank God she is saved! I politely parked my van and said "babies you don't move, Mommy is going in! Staci says, "Mom are you going to let that mean lady get away with that?" "Staci baby, you just hang tight let Mommy handle this." (Sidebar; your babies watch your every move; they watch what you do and say). So, I go inside I say, "Ma'am I need to speak with the Manager on Duty." He came from the back, and I said, "Sir your employee just chunked my money, and the coins hit me in my head. I have my children in the car and she did this in front of them! He's looking at me very strangely, like "Ok, and your point is?" The boldness is rising in me. I exclaimed, "Sir you have no idea who I am, I will own this place. You have messed with the wrong one. I am the King's daughter!" That was the beginning of the launch of Extremities Salon and Day Spa!

I have my answer, and now I have my location, but not before one more move. Remember the sweet Doctor I was telling you about? He leased another salon to us. He said to me you have been a good tenant even when you didn't have to; you kept up on the rent and utilities. We are going to move you to another one of our locations. I will have the maintenance man move you there until your own salon is ready." Can someone say He will fix it every time! I am not sure of the length of the process of buying and the renovations, but God's favor to me is better than I could ever explain. The property owner certainly did not have to help. He was not obligated, but I am so glad He did. I can't explain how hard this is, but if you are going to make any moves, please be wise. Take counsel from someone that has been there. God always has a witness. For the next several months, it was consistent work. We worked around the clock as the salon emerged. I cannot begin to tell you, but I want my experience to be one that can forever help anyone that reads my story.

Your Thoughts

Chapter 7

No Paycheck

"When God blesses you financially don't raise your standard of living, raise your standard of giving" (Mark Batterson).

With great excitement, we are now prepared to move into 1705 North Salisbury Boulevard. Can somebody say, "The dream has finally become a reality!" The long nights, the tears, the frustrations, and the disappointments have brought us to a place of victory. I had so many emotions going through my heart simultaneously. I'm nervous, I'm happy, but most of all I am extremely grateful for the Lord's favor, and trust, it was on and poppin'. People were coming from everywhere just to see these two young African Americans in their early thirty's, in Salisbury MD doing something that had never been done. We were situated on a major highway. Look at God! Everything He gave us was top of the line. We had designers from Belvedere come down to take my vision out of my head and make it pure reality! Who would have known this but God? Who could do this but God? Who could have opened this door but God? Kaile and I found favor with the USDA, and our working relationship was just wonderful. We could trust them. They supported our vision and always offered sound advice. We birthed so many community outreach organizations out of that building. We started working with the Middle Schools. Being a philanthropist was my favorite. Just to see the look on the young ladies faces as they shared their desires and passion was priceless. I remember all the girls trying to share their ideas simultaneously, and I am saying, "wait, girls, one at a time."

Giving back means so much. There is more satisfaction in giving than always being on the receiving end. We birthed "Extremities School of the Arts" in Spring 2007. We started with five students full of motivation, vision, and dreams. We did so once a year. Joe, Trisha, Kaile, and I worked hard to give the students the latest materials to help them sharpen their skills and believe in themselves. We wanted to help expand their businesses and their dreams. Some went on to open their own salons, and some moved by faith and expanded their existing ones. God blessed us, and we were able to give full graduations at Salisbury University. Each graduation was catered for the graduates and their families. We wanted to be a blessing, and we never reaped a dime financially. Let me say this; it takes finances to make things happen, and God kept the four of us, and we never gave up. We never gave less than the best. We wanted the confidence of each student to soar! I want to say as a sidebar, Kaile and I have so much love and respect for Joe and Trish. No matter what, they never stopped giving. They believed with us, had faith and endured with us. They showed up each Monday as if they were getting paid a million bucks. Needless to say, there was no monetary gain, but the joy and excitement we experienced watching the students grasping new ideas, new purpose, and a new direction were priceless. To God be the glory!

We are called to serve, not to be served. Listen, for twelve years we worked hard to maintain what God had given us. I often heard things people were saying about us and sometimes it could be disturbing. If they only knew our story! For five years, I went back and forth concerning this book but now is the time. My daughter said to me, "Mom finish your book; someone needs this story. Someone needs the truth so they can live and be free from bondage."

We had many good times in that salon; from parties to church, or just sharing and motivating each other. We had entrepreneurs working with us, and there was never a dull moment. However, people had it all wrong; the glamor of it all came with great pressure. The more God gives you, the harder things can get. I cannot begin to tell you how many days Kaile and I had to encourage each other. I am so blessed that God gave us each other because if not, I just don't know how we would have made it. The more people you have to manage can sometimes bring more drama and confusion. We wanted freedom, unity, and love, but that is not always the case. There were so many weeks and days we worked and just barely made it. Our overhead was a whopping $19,000 in expenses each month. There was absolutely no room for error. He's so faithful. We are still standing by the grace of God, so at this point right here, somebody, please help me bless God for our sanity and His amazing strength. When we think of his goodness, that alone should make you dance. Don't be stuck on what you see; get stuck on who you know!

Some say it is crazy to run a business and not be paid, and I know that I have mentioned this before. How did you pay your bills? How did you run your personal life? I will expound on that more in the upcoming chapters. It's certainly by His grace! Even with the staff we had, their rent only covered about 30% of our expenses. I never wanted to overburden my staff. I wanted to see them make it; so for years we went without! There is nobody like our God. He would often use people to bless us, and He knew right when to send them because it was always on time. I was reading Bishop Noel's book, and he made a very profound statement. He said: "Jesus broke all the rules in order to bless those that needed a blessing; regardless of the thoughts of man He had a plan!" Remember I said earlier, "God taught us every step of the way. Everything we needed, He did it."

I decided to go back to school again. This would be my second time attending D.C.U. (Dudley's Cosmetology University). I wanted to enhance my skills and expand my knowledge base. I have always had a love for hair and its scientific makeup. Needless to say, all the degrees in the world can never teach you like experience. Real life experience can teach us how to be better and find new ways to enhance our abilities. I must add, we had so many good times that I could never concentrate on our bad times. The good always outweighed the bad!

I was raised in a home full of love and faith, and we learned how to block out the negative. God will truly sustain your thoughts if you let him, even in the midst of a drought. That's exactly why we never looked like our story! Never underestimate the power of love, faith, and prayer. God will show up and meet you right where you are. He loves us with our flaws.

I want to share a good time with you. I remember one day we were in the salon, and a young lady came in with a hearing impediment. Poor Joseph didn't know what to do, and the irony of it all was that there was so much laughter. Not because the young lady could not hear, but he was carrying on a full conversation, and she was not answering a word. He looks at me (our stations were adjacent so I could clearly see}; I was trying so hard to keep my laughs in. He's sweating and looking at me and at this point, I could not contain myself! Joseph says, Marie, what is wrong with this lady? She acts as if she cannot hear. I said, "She can't," and everyone laughs. Now don't think by any means we are laughing at the disability, but can you picture this young man saying: "Ma'am, are you ok, Ma'am do you like your hair, with no response? Those were fun times, good times, and blessed times.

Early 2010 things began to change; we could not put in enough hours. Every week, things got harder and every month the frustration of it all came tumbling down like bricks! Here we go, the struggle is now real; we just can't fight anymore. Our strength is diminishing, and the bank is asking us to upgrade our contracts. The market is down, and the salon is upside down. Lord, what do we do? We have lives at stake, how God? What do you do when God is silent? I wanted to cry myself to sleep, but my faith and trust in God would not let me punk out. Let's go on with life as usual leave this battle up to God!

We began planning our biggest event of the century; Extremities Extravaganza. Extremities Extravaganza was a huge black tie affair, and tickets were selling like wildfire and everyone was purchasing their evening gowns. I am yet rejoicing even in the struggle because we just received a good report that Dad is cancer free! Wow, no time for fretting, no time for crying over our struggles, Gods' got it! We were exhausted, but God was not. Whose report will you believe!

Your Thoughts

Chapter 8

The Survival

Do you trust me when my answer is wait?

It is now the end of 2011, and the bank is now demanding an answer. "Mr. and Mrs. Turner, We will give you until the end of the business day to make a decision." Remember earlier I asked, "What do we do when God is silent?" Well, the next morning I rose early and began to go before the Lord. He immediately speaks and directed me to Joshua 9. He says "make no deals with the enemy, sign nothing." "Ok God, I trust you. Man has failed me, but you never let me down." I went to the salon early in the morning and, a good pastor friend of mine was waiting to receive service. She says, "Rie, I heard the Lord say He's going to move you. Now listen, I had never shared a word of this with her. Only my hubby, and I knew what we were faced with! No, no, no, no, that's the last thing I wanted to hear. I want them to make it right. Surely, the USDA can fix this! No, God wants to free you and Kaile. Ok God, whatever you do is well, but please show us, please direct us. There has to be deliverance and who would have ever known that help was really on the way!

We are now into 2012; the postman walks in and hands me a letter. It is from the bank. What strength He gives us in the midst of the storm! He is not going to let us go down like this. It's a Thursday, and there is a shop full of people. Imagine smiling in the midst of pain; what an emotional moment. All I knew was that I was His child and He has this building. Lord, please make them do right by us. We are your children, we are seeds of righteousness. I am screaming inside, what's going on, yet God says "trust me, just trust me. Keep your mouth closed, listen for my instructions and trust me." Please know this, God never gives us the entire story, He only gives us part. He said He was going to free us.

Now at this point, there are so many different things being said, hurtful things, and letters circulating; all this right under our nose. I wanted to defend our family so badly, but the God of all grace said: "keep your mouth closed!" Why God are you letting my enemies triumph over me? We have faith. We have treated people right; Lord be our help! He may not come when you want Him, but He is always on time.

Please believe, I don't care how saved you are, or how much you love God, you are human. You have feelings; you bleed just like everyone else! We can be very emotional beings sometimes. Our emotions can cause us to react to our current circumstance. Let's learn to stand still because baby listen, when you wait; He will make everything right for you. Oh yes, I am a living witness. Here is another awesome place to bless His Name!

At this point, the bank decided to take over unbeknownst to our team; but it's all good! When I should be crying, I really felt relieved! The most hurtful thing is that God's people should be praying for each other instead of talking. You never know, I am for real, you never know.

As the months and days went by, I was trying to come to grips with what to do! My sweet husband is such a no nonsense man. He is so carefree that even if something were bothering him, we would never know! He is always saying, "Have faith baby. I don't know how, but God has this."

I really had a heart for the people. I wanted everyone to be ok; I certainly felt like we let our community down, even God, but the Bible says to lift up your head, oh ye gates! Yes Lord, yes, I feel my help coming! Depression, guilt, and sadness, you cannot live here! I am a child of the King.

One Sunday afternoon we visited Tabernacle of Prayer for a Family and Friend's day, and my family sat together; I said Lord let the word minister to us in our low season! In a whisper, God said, "I am the Lord that healeth thee, I send my word to heal!" The man of God calls out our entire family and says, "God said keep your mouth closed, He's fighting for you." Thank you Jesus! I was at a breaking point. Was anyone praying for us? Was anyone holding up our arms? When I can get past the pain of the loss of a dream, I can begin to see things in the spiritual realm. I turned to God and said, "You are the only one who could handle this mantle. This business has been a lot for us, and you upheld us all the way. Who could have been able to handle such a great expense without you? Twelve years, twelve long years."

Sometimes people laugh at my praise, but I must say this, keep on laughing; I must keep praising! We were not demoted we were promoted! Now listen, it took a minute to come to grips with all this. We suffered the loss of friendships, partnerships, and fellowship but we didn't lose anything we never really had. True true love and friendship are not predicated only on good times, but love is consistent. A friend loves at all times. Proverbs 17:17.

The new owners thought they had two young Black dummies, and I almost fell for it. Had I fell for that, I would have never been free. I am using it at this point because my husband said: "baby whatever you want is cool with me." The contract said $2,400 a month for rent; you pay land taxes, maintenance fees, and trash removal, and I said ok. Then she tells me; you pay me a $7,000 deposit! Do I look like boo-boo the fool? God will make you shift, release it and let it go.

Now we have people proclaiming to speak prophetically saying, "The Lord says for me to tell you to stay." However, remember, the Lord said just trust me. This is that moment I need you to trust me! Hold on; help is on the way. Someone right now reading this book is holding on to save face for people. God is saying let it go; there are seasons, and we need to know when that season is over and praise Him for what He has already done. I cannot fathom in my mind why our trial had to be so extreme, but what I do know is that peace and joy are here. We never know how distraught we are until our deliverance comes.

Chapter 9

The Truth Is

"You know the truth by the way it feels" (author unknown)

Seven hundred fifty thousand dollars ($750,000) from barely having debt to having debt, but it's all good, it's called life! I would not take back anything that I have been through. It was all purposeful, and I have learned so much. Let me say this; I wear a size nine shoe it fits me perfect. God already knew my makeup, He made me, I am here on purpose, and for a purpose; I am not a mistake. My failures do not identify my purpose. My failures identify my strength! *The Truth Is,* God chooses whomever He wants to get the task complete. We were public spectacles for a reason. There were days when I felt our family story was on every billboard in Salisbury. The truth is, no one knew this, but my bankers fought hard behind the scenes. I didn't mention this earlier; we had two mortgages, electric, land taxes, gas, water bills, and the list goes on. We didn't get to take vacations because we simply could not afford to; our focus was maintaining.

In late 2007, the Lord did bless us to refinance our home; this was before the market crashed and homes lost value. That was the best. There's always the calm before the storm, and we were able to finally experience some freedom, because stress will kill you. Our babies had a real Christmas, and we had so much fun vacationing in Florida. We were carefree for that moment, good sleep, family, and love. Amazing, simply amazing. Lord don't let this moment end. Well, all good things do; friend listen, I am not complaining, not for one second. I am honored to still have the favor of God even in the low places; there is not a moment that I don't. The Bible says "in all thy ways acknowledge Him, and He will direct your path. Proverbs 3:6.

Days and nights have gone by, and I had rode by the old salon on 13 and asked God why? Why did you fulfill such a dream and allow us to lose it? This is what He gave me; "It was for a season. Ecclesiastes 3:6 was an enlightening scripture to me and at the end of the day, God does have a plan. There is a purpose for your pain and there's purpose for your disappointment. Don't be ashamed or afraid; God has better.

Don't weep over what was another day. Rise up, fight, push, challenge yourself. Now let's put praise right there.

I am so blessed that my children are so awesome, even with our flaws they loved their parents. They didn't always know this, but they have always been our motivation. They are going to be greater than we are. Why? Because God said so.

As we were moving to our new location, and releasing the past, something very magical happened. Some of the people who once were talking were now apologizing for their actions. "Marie we love you and Kaile; I am so sorry for not trusting God with you. Hallelujah! God promised us that He never fails. I have never seen the righteous forsaken nor his seed begging bread. Psalms 37:25.

Let me ask this question: "Do you know who you really are?" Do you know who really loves you? Do you know who really keeps you? You are not alone; He loves you. *The Truth Is*; this test, this trial, is only for a moment. We made it; we survived and you will too!

Your Thoughts

Chapter 10

The Freedom

"Joy does not simply happen to us, we have to choose joy and keep choosing it every day" (Henry Drummond).

We have spent some very precious time together, and I am so honored. (All smiles). We are at a victory stretch, and we are moving for our last time. Extremities Salon has been everywhere, but its all good and purposeful.

721 Roland Street here we come, and I am in the middle of a crisis. A the young lady at our church was murdered. No way, this is not happing. God, please let this be a joke, please let's stop what we are doing and pray. She is a good woman, Lord help!

In the midst of this test, as we were preparing for a shift, my realtor calls and said, "Marie, I have a building for you." My reply to Matt was "at this point I can't, my hubby is at the hospital with our babies from the church; they lost their Mom this morning." He says, "Marie, I heard that on the news, but if you get a second, I believe you will like this location I found." My mind is going in circles, He promised us not to put more on us than we can bear, but Lord, this is heavy.

At this point, there are floods of people coming to the hospital. The children have so much company at this point; my hubby said "lets take 5 minutes to go see the building," I reply Ok. Not even walking completely in the building I said "absolutely not, it's a negative," and I walk out. No sooner than I get out the door, the Lord said I need you to look again! Oh gosh, Lord you are taking us from the palace to the pit; to the slum. I cannot Jesus. Kaile is standing in the middle of the floor talking to the new landlord who says, "If you want it, you can have it."

No sir, this is not what my clients are used to. However, the Lord says "look again." Standing there, He began to download vision. Before I knew it, I said we would take it! OMG did I just say that? Babe was like, "we will." Without a dime exchanged, nor a contract written, just favor, we accepted the contract. That young man didn't know us; he only knew of us. God factored in my failures, and our failures do not stop our future. Wait one minute let me dance; I can't contain the praise in my feet.

There's absolutely no way I can live without Him! My sister, Evangelist Fooks, reminded me of that in the middle of my pain I could not stop my God-given assignments. Someone still needed me, and I need them to survive. We are finally in a place where things are settling down we can finally breathe! My new landlord is amazing and so calming. Finally, someone that's not a bully, and he places value on the gifts inside of us. He says we are all out here trying to make it, and we need each other. Why in the world has no one else in my past grasped that?

For the next several months, we were getting settled and finding peace and comfort. I can finally relax and enjoy being a business owner. The stress of it all is lifting, and my electric bill is amazing. I had never seen a $400 bill for business. Wow. Our atmosphere was pleasant with soft music, and good conversations. The atmosphere was warm and inviting, and my clients loved their new home! Treat people the way you want to be treated, love and respect given, is love and respect received! Garnett was always there to the rescue when my hubby needed a friend to be there. They would get stuff done. He could pick up the phone, and he would be there in a flash. It's funny because everyone knows how anal I am when it comes to cleanliness. I need all things in order. Things are only getting better now, and I am entering into the fulfillment of the promise! I didn't say we have not had trials because we have, but God matured us, and He settled us. After a while, you can face the storm with a new level of expectation. You know that if He did it before He will do it again!

We have gotten through some gloomy days with grace. Let me tell you this friend; God will have you do some of the things that will require total faith and trust. I was instructed to cut back my schedule, and I thought, Lord if I cut back anymore there would be nothing left. When I tell my husband this, he will think I am tripping, but he didn't. He said "Ok."

I want you to understand that nothing that has happened in our lives has been planned out. If I knew for one moment that God was going to transition my life in so many different facets, I would have asked some questions! He says go, I go. He says cut back, I do. I know some felt that I was totally out of my mind. Some even wondered, "How are they making it?" Kaile and Marie have something special; it's called faith and substance.

In late 2014, my husband's BMW was hit as we were preparing for his Men's Conference. He came out the hotel only to find the front end of his truck bashed in. Kaile Turner was so calm. And what's so funny about that is he is extremely particular about his vehicles. He takes good care of what we have, and anyone who knows us knows that. They are fully aware that we drive our vehicles until there is no more life. Therefore, when our truck went in the shop the rental company gave us a 2015 Tahoe. I had forgotten how nice it was to have a big truck again! I was afraid to drive it at first, but Lord, why did you let me ride in this smooth truck. The seats just took me in; Lord have mercy! So the girl that was once whining now wants to buy this.

"Baby, can we get this truck? Please find out how we can buy this." "What are you serious?"

"Yes, I am in love with truck, it is so smooth." "Ok, I am going to see what we can do."

So we go to the Dealership, and I am very excited. For real, it's been so long, and I wanted to know for sure if we do, or we don't. Lord, what are your thoughts. If it's not your will, close the door and if it is, make it easy. I am sharing this because I have another point to make. The salesman came out and said "Mr. Turner, do you really like that truck?" Kaile says, "yes, my wife does." This is the kicker; the payment will be $1,100. "That's a negative; let's go baby." We gathered our things and left. There's nothing crazy about us, let's truly ask God for direction in all we do. I said all of that to say this; our salesman brought out a 2011Tahoe with low mileage, one owner, and it was garage kept. He said (Mrs. Turner) it is in your price range. I said I want what I want, but God gave me what I needed!

Often we beg for something and God just lets us have it even when He sees down the road.

In early January 2015, our church went on a fast; and I went into this fast with an open mind and heart, and the Lord began to deal with me. Here we go again; He says do you trust me? God knows I do. After all, I have been through, I am open to whatever at this point, not knowing what was coming next. He says, "I am pulling you from your job." Say what Lord?" He reminded me of what had been spoken in times past; He says, "I have need of you." Ok God show me, lead me, and I will follow. Now I have to break this news to my hubby. He's always been supportive, so why am I nervous about telling him! One thing I know for sure is that if the Lord speaks to me, He will definitely deal with him as well! When I sat down to talk with this amazing man, he says, "baby, you know I support you, and I trust that God will provide for us!" That very day the Lord reiterated, "do you trust me," and I said "Lord I do." That same day a good friend came by my home and said I have something for you. Ok, I replied. She came in, all smiles and said "Marie; you have been such a blessing to me, thanks. She puts $100 in my hand and leaves. When I opened my hand, the tears would not stop flowing. God knew exactly what I needed. It wasn't about the money; it was about the confirmation. After meeting our weekly expenses, I only had a few dollars left and the Lord spoke to me and said: "I need you to trust me." I cried the entire afternoon because if I never knew it before, I knew that day that my Heavenly Father loves me. There is nobody like my God!

I am embarking on a completely new life and there are so many things that I have before the Lord, and so many questions. How will we survive financially? Trust in the Lord with all your heart! We are preparing for our revival, and I am asking God to please speak to me through His Word. I certainly don't need anyone to lay hands on me, but speak Lord for your servant hears. So much confirmation came in those three days that I felt strengthened, free in my spirit, and light on my feet. So God now that you have given me direction and clarity, when do I tell my clients? I have so much love and respect for them, and we have been family. They have watched our children grow as I have watched some of them marry and have their own children we have a bond!

The transition is not easy; being obedient is not either, especially when you don't know the full plan. I am at peace. My customers are sad, but they understand that it's our time. When I told my Daddy, he made a huge joke out of it all. Now, I have been styling hair for 27 years, over half my life! I never knew what it was like not to work or have my own, but it is time. Daddy said, "Baby you have another ten years," and I replied, "Not!" I don't want to be old and broke down!

In the midst of transition, another huge opportunity came my way. I received an email from the US Trichology Institute, and I had my client read it; I asked her to call the Institute directly. She came back and said "Rie Rie, it's not a joke! I said how in the world did they get my information? I immediately directed her to Kaile to get our bankcard, and I said: "pay them I'm going!"

I had waited for this opportunity for years, and I'm still in awe. When I got to my intake class, I asked my instructor, out of curiosity, how he got my information. I had applied to the school years ago when I thought I had a shot, but my Dad got sick, and things in my life changed temporarily. When your loved one is going through, you have to be available. Certainly, my parents are a priority!

So let's get back to my Instructor. She said your name came up in our National Database as one of the top salons in your area. Look at God! Everything is about timing. I was so honored that God saw fit to see about me. I was able to pass my intake and was able to move on to the next level, which is a Certified Hair Loss Practitioner. How awesome is that? The course was very intense. It was three days of power packed information. Now I can offer something different to those in need of hair restoration. Lord, you're mighty. I can give sick men and women hope again, and lift someone's spirits in the middle of their adversity. Now that is amazing! I did tell God this; I want a facility that enables those that don't have the resources to come and receive services and it's going to happen. Every delay is not a denial.

The year 2015 was a very impactful year. Did I tell you how my family and friends pulled together and paid my full tuition, and my hotel expenses? He is a marvelous God! There's no way in the world that I could live without my God. He allowed me to retain the information in order to pass my finals.

We were in a board meeting at church, and I had not made my announcement of what the Lord said in September; only a few people knew. Our Bishop said, "I am installing Marie as our Pastor." Oh no Lord. Then he replies, "We will be doing this in September." Lord, have mercy. My Dad did not know that the Lord said September for retirement. So now I am trying to settle my spirit, this is too much! Pastor T; please tell me this is not real. She replies "Marie listen, God called you just like you are. There is no manual that goes with this assignment."

Well, here we go, all things in motion. September came, and my nerves were totally shot. The practice wasn't open, but the salon was closing. I could not find a soul to carry on the legacy. Honestly, I could care less. I had already started giving everything I had away! "Oh my God," the look on Mr. Turners face; he said, "Baby you give away everything; sell this stuff." I said "absolutely not" (in my child-like voice), the Lord said to give, and I am going to listen! The smiles on the faces of the customers were as if they were shopping at Macys. Still not really knowing His plans and direction, I continued to move forward. Whatever you do, never become stagnate keep going by faith. Psalms 37:23.

When I attended a conference Pastor T. was hosting, I had been in prayer due to the fact I wanted my girls to be okay. I didn't want them to work for someone that was not going to love them as we did. When I walked into the service, the presence of God was already there. The woman of God began to preach and says to me; "God said do not close the salon." Wow God! My landlord was good at first then he said, "Marie if you're not going to be here, I do not want anyone else." Therefore, he gave my girls a deadline to move out, I was already gone. My transition had already taken place.

It's all happening now. God made provision for the girls, and I was ever so grateful. They are all settled and in a good place, and now it's my turn, or so I thought. I figured once they were in a good place I could open my practice and take care of my clients and be free. The Lord did free me. However, we no longer had the hustle and bustle of that end of the business, and I could now enjoy my life and experience freedom. God's ways are not our ways, and our thoughts are not His, for He has a plan.

My girls surprised me with a retirement party. I thought I was going to faint seeing all the people, feeling all the love and support, all the appreciative ladies showering me with love; it was all so overwhelming! The girls did that, and the mother in me was so off. I was worried about them being jammed up. They looked at me and was like "Mrs. Marie, we got this." I love them; my children rock!

Since I have been off the floor, my first two weeks I was having a ball. Then I looked at our finances. I said to myself, "Ok Marie, you have to bring it in and be wise." Remember, you are not working, Lord, reality sat in. I started to think about how I was going to be able to do my girlie things; but don't you know, I am doing it. No, the practice didn't open when I wanted it to because the contract on the building I wanted fell through. It was ok; I don't ever want to be in bondage again, and I wasn't signing up for that. When you experience freedom, you do not go back; so I will wait. I'm good. We are not prying open any doors now, and that's growth for me, guys. When I want something done, I will work extra to make it happen.

This has been the year of events for us, but I must say I am good. God has shown Himself mighty, and we have been taking our journey one day at a time! We are pastoring the ministry that God had given my Dad to establish in 1995. God has blessed the ministry to be very progressive and full of youth and life. My parents have been pillars in our community and are still vibrant examples and mentors to many!

Let me say this, whatever God has for you shall come to pass. My journey has been long, but its been strong. He's molding us and making us. I do not care what you do in this life, just remember that only what you do for Christ will last. Hold on; help is on the way. I love you! He is a keeper, and He has got you covered. Don't quit, don't throw in the towel. Fight, scream, pray and fight some more. *The Truth is*; God knows you already have the victory!

"When you feel overwhelmed and you are tempted to take everything into your own hands, you have to make yourself be still. The battle is not yours, the battle is the Lord's. Give it to God!"

Your Thoughts

Printed in the United States
By Bookmasters